Spot the Differences
Bee or Wasp?

by Adeline J. Zimmerman

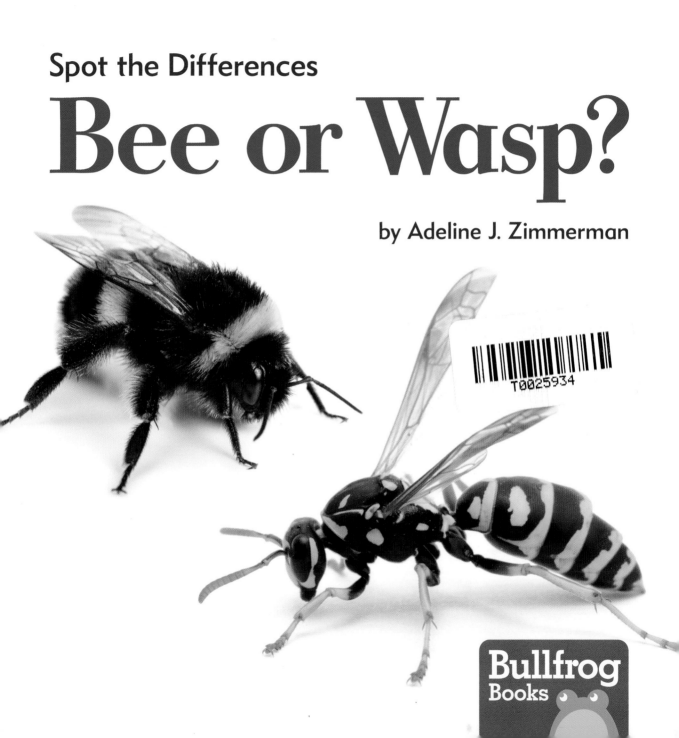

Bullfrog Books

Ideas for Parents and Teachers

Bullfrog Books let children practice reading informational text at the earliest reading levels. Repetition, familiar words, and photo labels support early readers.

Before Reading

- Discuss the cover photo. What does it tell them?

- Look at the picture glossary together. Read and discuss the words.

Read the Book

- "Walk" through the book and look at the photos. Let the child ask questions. Point out the photo labels.

- Read the book to the child, or have him or her read independently.

After Reading

- Prompt the child to think more. Ask: Have you ever seen a bee or a wasp? If so, where was the insect? What was it doing?

Bullfrog Books are published by Jump!
5357 Penn Avenue South
Minneapolis, MN 55419
www.jumplibrary.com

Copyright © 2022 Jump! International copyright reserved in all countries. No part of this book may be reproduced in any form without written permission from the publisher.

Library of Congress Cataloging-in-Publication Data

Names: Zimmerman, Adeline J., author.
Title: Bee or wasp? / by Adeline J. Zimmerman.
Description: Bullfrog books.
Minneapolis, MN: Jump!, Inc., [2022]
Series: Spot the differences
Includes index. | Audience: Ages 5–8
Identifiers: LCCN 2021028542 (print)
LCCN 2021028543 (ebook)
ISBN 9781636903378 (hardcover)
ISBN 9781636903385 (paperback)
ISBN 9781636903392 (ebook)
Subjects: LCSH: Bees—Juvenile literature.
Wasps—Juvenile literature.
Classification: LCC QL565.2 .Z56 2022 (print)
LCC QL565.2 (ebook)
DDC 595.79/9—dc23
LC record available at https://lccn.loc.gov/2021028542
LC ebook record available at https://lccn.loc.gov/2021028543

Editor: Jenna Gleisner
Designer: Michelle Sonnek

Photo Credits: irin-k/Shutterstock, cover, 1 (right), 21; DieterMeyrl/iStock, 1 (left); Paul Reeves Photography/Shutterstock, 3, 6–7 (bottom), 12–13; MMCez/Shutterstock, 4; PhotoRR/Shutterstock, 5; Jack Hong/Shutterstock, 6–7 (top), 23tr; Luc Pouliot/Shutterstock, 8–9; Akil Rolle-Rowan/Shutterstock, 10–11; Isarat/Shutterstock, 14–15, 23tl; Franz Christoph Robiller/imageBROKER/SuperStock, 16–17; Irina Kozorog/Shutterstock, 18–19, 23br; Antagain/iStock, 20; Shutterstock, 22 (left); Mircea Costina/Shutterstock, 22 (right), 23bl; Emagnetic/Shutterstock, 24 (top); Petrica75/Shutterstock, 24 (bottom).

Printed in the United States of America at Corporate Graphics in North Mankato, Minnesota.

Table of Contents

How to Use This Book

In this book, you will see pictures of both bees and wasps. Can you tell which one is in each picture?

Hint: You can find the answers if you flip the book upside down!

This is a bee.

4

This is a wasp.

Both are insects.
They look alike.
But they are
not the same.

Can you spot
the differences?

stripe

Both are black.

Bees have gold stripes.

Wasps have bright yellow ones.

Which is this?

Bees are hairy.
Wasps are shiny.
Which is this?

Bees are round.

Wasps are thin.

Which is this?

Bees make hives.

Wasps make nests.

Who lives here?

◀····· honeycomb

15

wing

Bees fly.

So do wasps.

A wasp's legs
hang down.

A bee's do not.

Which is this?

A bee stings once.

Wasps sting many times.

Which is this?

Look out!

stinger

See and Compare

antenna

hairy body

round body

gold stripes

two pairs of wings

stinger

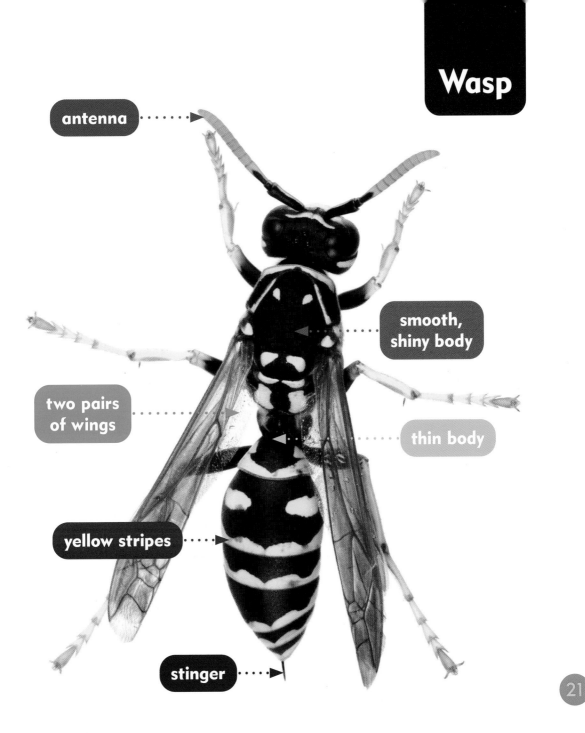

Wasp

antenna

smooth, shiny body

two pairs of wings

thin body

yellow stripes

stinger

Quick Facts

Bees and wasps are both insects. They both have three pairs of legs, two pairs of wings, and three main body parts. They are similar, but they have differences. Take a look!

Bees
- make hives
- make honey
- can only sting one time

Wasps
- make nests
- do not make honey
- can sting many times

Picture Glossary

hives
Homes for swarms of bees.

insects
Small animals with three pairs of legs, one or two pairs of wings, and three main body parts.

nests
Papery shelters built by wasps to live in.

stings
Pierces or wounds with a small, sharp point.

Index

To Learn More

Finding more information is as easy as 1, 2, 3.

❶ Go to www.factsurfer.com

❷ Enter "beeorwasp?" into the search box.

❸ Choose your book to see a list of websites.